VERY SUPERSTITIOUS

A BLACK SUPERSTITION COLORING BOOK

CONCEPT BY: AMANDA CHAMBERS

ILLUSTRATIONS BY: MYNECIA STEELE

ISBN-13: 978-1-7340913-4-2

Very Superstitious: The Black Superstition Coloring Book

Proudly self-published through Divine Legacy Publishing, LLC. www.divinelegacypublishing.com

DEDICATION

This coloring book is dedicated to the women who taught me all about superstitions: my grandmother Dolores Rice, my great grandmother Dorothy Young, and my other great grandmother Frances Rice. These women did not play with me when it came to superstitions, and you best believe that I have carried on the tradition.

AUTHORS NOTE

First, I must give a HUGE shout out to my illustrator, Mynecia "Mya" Steele. When I tell you this woman is talented and amazing, I'm serious! I'm convinced she's magical . . . like, literal Black Girl Magic. Thank you, Mya, for putting up with all my crazy ideas and sprinkling all your Black Girl Magic on all of my projects. I couldn't bring my vision to life without you. Y'all, go check her out at www.thisismyne.com. You will not be disappointed, I promise!

My mother taught me to color when I was about 2 or 3, and I haven't stopped since. I was coloring for fun and stress relief before the big adult coloring movement of the last decade or so. But, like most mainstream movements, there aren't a lot of coloring books that focus on aspects of Black culture. I'm not saying everything has to be all Black all the time (but also I would be perfectly content if it was), but why can't we color things that are relevant to our unique culture? Why can't we color images that look like us?

Well, I'm making it my business to create coloring books that are relevant to Black folks that make us smile, laugh, and remember good times. Very Superstitious is the first in a line of coloring books that focus on all things Black, so be on the lookout for more in the months and years to come.

Finally, in the back of the book, you will find a page for you to write down what you think each superstition is. If you're stuck trying to figure out what one of the superstitions are, a master list can be found on my website at www.amandamchambers.com/superstitionlist. Also, there are three color test pages in the very back of the book so you can test out colors to decide which ones you want to use as you color your way through the book.

Happy coloring!

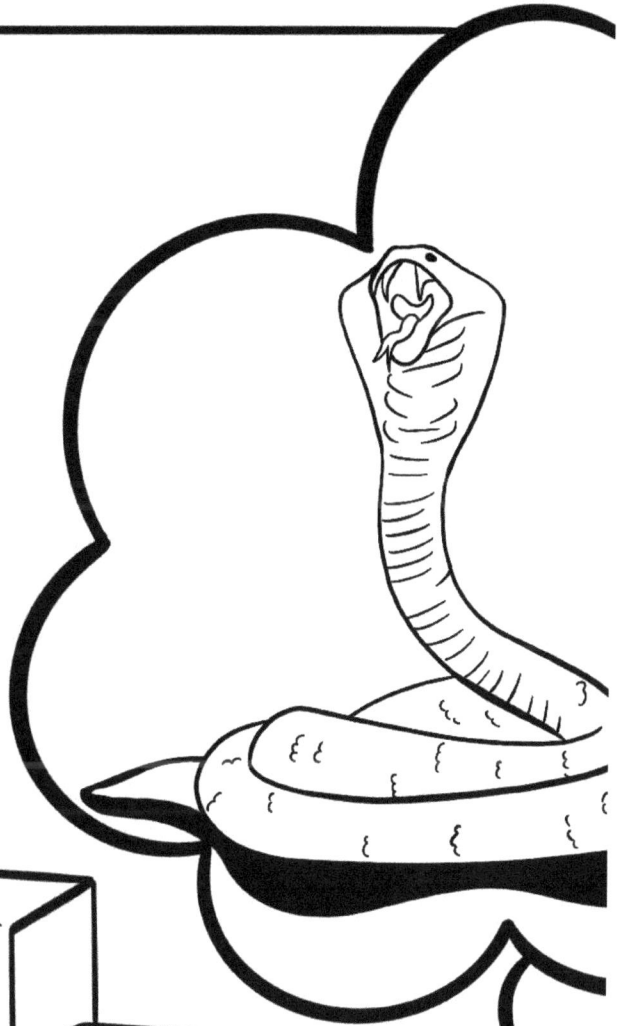

HICCUP!

HICCUP!

HICCUP!

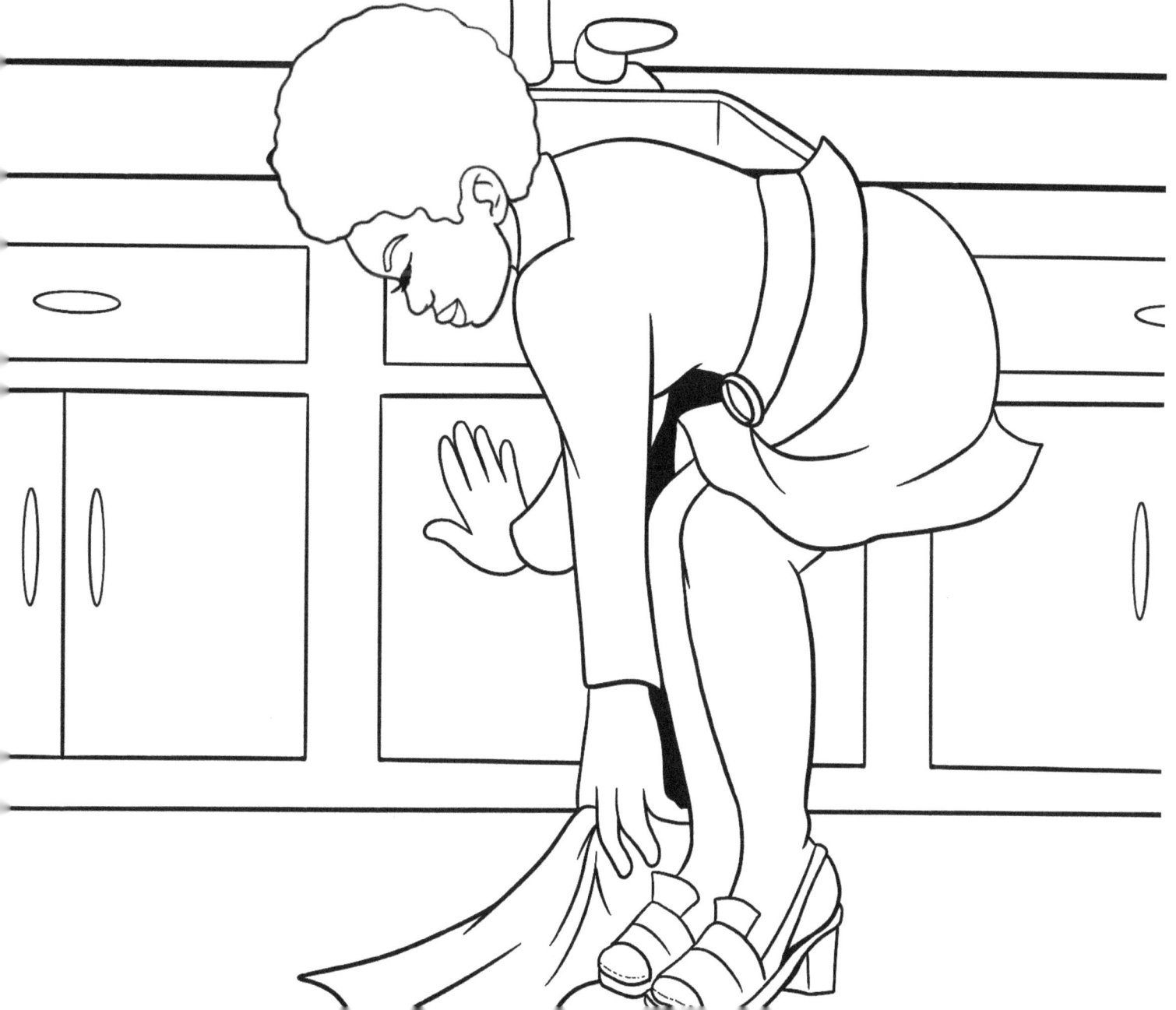

WRITE GUESSES HERE

_____
_____
_____
_____
_____
_____
_____
_____
_____
_____
_____
_____
_____
_____
_____
_____
_____
_____
_____

THANKS FOR PURCHASING THIS BOOK!

Your support means the world to me.

There's more to come . . .

To find out when the newest coloring book is available, or to learn more about my children's books and romance novels (yes, I write both), please visit my website www.amandamchambers.com and sign up for my newsletter. Not only will you be the first to find out when new books come out, but I'll also send out one free coloring page a month. Newsletters only go out once a month because, honestly, that's all I have time for, so you don't have to worry about being spammed with a million emails from me.

You can also keep up with me on social media using the info below:

Instagram: @amandachamberssays
Facebook: Amanda Chambers
Twitter: @achamberssays
YouTube: Amanda Chambers Says
TikTok: @amandachamberssays

COLOR TEST PAGE

COLOR TEST PAGE